Meadow Ghost

Claudia Bunce

BookLeaf
Publishing

India | USA | UK

Meadow Ghost © 2022 Claudia Bunce

All rights reserved.

No part of this publication may be reproduced, stored in a retrieval system, or transmitted, in any form or by any means, electronic, mechanical, photocopying, recording or otherwise, without the prior written permission of the presenters.

Claudia Bunce asserts the moral right to be identified as author of this work.

Presentation by *BookLeaf Publishing*

Web: www.bookleafpub.com

E-mail: info@bookleafpub.com

ISBN: 978-81-962188-8-1

First edition 2022

PREFACE

I was inspired by a number of films and fairy
tales, and I think I should mention them here.

The Perfect Couple is inspired by the Bluebeard
fairy tale and the legends surrounding Countess
Elizabeth Bathory.

Artemis 81 is a cut up poem using some
dialogue from the 1981 BBC TV movie of the
same name, written by David Rudkin and
Alastair Reid. The White Reindeer is inspired by
the Finnish film of the same name directed by
Erik Blomberg, and written by Blomberg and
Mirjami Kuosmanen, which itself is inspired by
Sami folk legends.

Dangers of Time is inspired by the documentary
Woodlands Dark and Days Bewitched directed
by Keir-la Janisse.

Blodeuwedd's Song is inspired by the Welsh
myth of Blodeuwedd, retold in the Mabinogion.
The Death of Jezebel is inspired by the woman
of the same name from the Bible, and Pandora's
Descendant is inspired by the Greek myth of
Pandora's Box. Great Goat God is inspired by

most occult descriptions of Baphomet, a deity that was adopted into new pagan.

Unbroken

Call me a witch,
The word does not hurt me.
I create my own fire
And I will not burn.

Push me down deeper,
Keep trying to drown me,
I will only swim free
But you never will learn.

Take a pin to my back,
I will not cry out in pain.
You want to rule over,
And make me feel small.

But I will never be controlled
By men's fake laws.
I am surrounded by sisters
Who won't let me fall.

We are the women
Who haunt your nightmares.
We speak the truths
You never want known.

We see your heart,
We know your anger,
We've seen your actions
And have survived your stones.

To all my friends out there
Lost in this world,
Let us be witches!
Let our tales be spoken!

Your soul is untamed
While your heart is unchained.
This is how I'm sure
We are unbroken!

The Perfect Couple

Oh dear, what can the matter be?
Bluebeard has married Elizabeth Bathory
They'll be happy in bloodlust for all of eternity,
Deep in the dark of their lair.

A match made in heaven,
(or more likely hell),
They would end up enabling
Each other so well.

Can't you see how happy they could be?

The countess craves blood,
Her husband wants control,
And maybe some murder
To cleanse out his soul.

While the countess bathes
Bluebeard shaves,
Then uses the razor
On a girl that they saved.

They'd laugh as the blood
Pours all over their heads,
Then they'd bask in its warmth

Together in bed.

Oh how happy they could be!

Sonnet

Please don't give your heart to me,
For hearts are easily broken.
Please don't speak you mind to me,
Some thoughts should remain unspoken.
Please don't promise me the moon,
Grand speeches mean nothing in the end.
Please don't compare me to the afternoon,
You shouldn't think you need to pretend.
Just remain here by my side
Til it's too late to say goodbye.

Artemis 81

He is haunted, heart shaped, and hungry.
His words shape your own coldest feeling,
You smile and are sad.
Take the pear,
Trust its flesh.
For all our sanity we must fall.

Silence
Free of history, insufficiently heard.
The sounds are holding her,
Footsteps echo back and forth.
They're in the air,
And all around we hear
A final harmony that shattered her.
A simple act can change a voice.

"What need in me so dark?"
My true self asks me.
I collect the morbid things,
Saving them from the beauty of humanity.
Why did I not cast you in the sea?
What horror is this you made me do?
And am I free?

The Willow-Cat

The willow-cat sprawls on the bank of the river
Lazing in the sun, letting life amble by.
She slowly dips her leaves in the gently
warming water,
Letting her paws brush the current as she lies.

The willow-cat stretches her branches in front of
her
And arches her back upwards to the sun,
Then rolls over to let the rays touch her belly,
Her green fur warming, as she smiles at no one.

Back and forth, back and forth, flicks her idle
tail,
Not a thing in this world could ever make her
stir.
Her roots keep her steady, and she closes her
eyes again.
The willow-cat goes back to sleep, with a deep
rustling purr.

Ikea

Getting lost in Ikea is like
Being in a nightmare designed by
Jacques Tati.
You bumble,
Innocently,
Through the store,
Not quite sure where you are,
In a state of pleasant confusion.
You can't find the end,
But the surroundings are so nice to look at.

It's not quite scary
But it is unsettling
How you can never find an exit.
You end up wandering
Around in this state of pleasant confusion,
A state that never changes.
You just keep going.
On and on and on,
Occasionally bumping into things,
And people,
Like Jacques Tati.

The Death of Jezebel

Jezebel put on her lipstick
Before her assassination,
(because when you're a political leader
it's not murder, it's an assassination)
She dared to go out on her own terms,
And was afterwards branded a whore
For maintaining her will.

Did you know she was a queen?
Queen of Israel, actually,
Originally from Phoenicia.
It seems like some people would like everyone
To forget that fact.
It's easier to judge a whore.

She was sent across countries
To marry a stranger.
In that situation,
Why shouldn't she bring something familiar
with her,
Like her faith?

Funny, how a god who preaches tolerance
Is the most intolerant of all.
Even her husband was more tolerant,
And when he was killed,
Overthrown in a religious war,
Jezebel lost her safety,
Her stability,
Her standing,
Everything that would protect her life.

She must have known that she
Was going to die,
And that knowledge removed her fear.
She gathered her own strength
And faced her enemies unafraid.

But only after her lipstick was perfect.

Lazy Sunday Haikus

Rainy day, inside
Snuggled up on the sofa
Under a blanket.

Hot tea with honey,
My hands wrapped around my mug,
Watching the outside.

Sun comes in brief spurts
Lighting up the rain drops so
They look like sunbeams,

Raining gold on the
Ground around the garden. Then
The clouds reappear.

The best place to be
When it rains on Sunday is
Underneath a cat.

Embracing Insomnia

Sometimes I find it hard to sleep.
I close my eyes,
Steady my breathing,
And try to drift off.
But sleep just passes me by
Like a runaway train.
So I lie in the dark waiting for nothing to
happen.

There isn't much to do
While you lie in the dark.
I tend to reminisce about past mistakes
And overthink any actions I took.
But it's better than what happens
When I do manage to drift off.

I don't like dreaming when I sleep.
I end up dreaming about reality.
Real places, real people,
But distorted,
Stretched into

A dream image of themselves
It's horrifying,
My own uncanny version of life.
Events twisted into a nightmare
That I can't control.

There are other dreams I have,
Dreams of falling
Down a shaft of light.
There's darkness around me
Except the path my body falls down.

The fall is slow,
Every breath of wind
I feel through every particle,
Every atom.
Back arched,
Head tossed,
Arms falling everywhere
As gravity moves me.
The air that surrounds me
Is as thick as water.
It buries me as I fall.
I always wake before I land.

I'd rather be awake forever
Than fall for eternity.

Chaos is a Woman

Chaos is a woman,
A maternal river that overflows
And floods the masculine roads.

Chaos watches silently
While men fight pointless battles
That always lead to innocent death.

Chaos is a woman,
One of great beauty and strength
Who enchants without even trying.

Chaos was taken unwillingly,
By a man who tried to tame her
And who then paid a most unfortunate price.

Chaos is a woman
Who creates life, such wondrous life,
Which then goes on to destroy

Chaos lives for her children
Who grow to love, protect, and revere her,
And are not afraid of violence or revenge.

Chaos is a woman

Who does not care if her children are not good.
She will always defend them when they call.

15

Chaos watches with amusement
As her children run wild and rampant,
While she dances in the plague.

Chaos is a woman
And not matter how hard men try
She will never be contained.

Pandora's Descendants

Cats are descendants of Pandora.
Think about it?
Pandora's story is a cautionary tale against
curiosity.
What killed the cat?
Curiosity.
Although cat's were brought back
By their own satisfaction.

Pandora was also intrigued by a box.
Where does a cat like to sit?
In a box.
What intrigues cats?
A small enclosed space they can explore.
In other words,
A box.

Depending on who you ask,
Cat's either bring bad luck or good.
Depending on which source you find,
Pandora either saves hope,
Or traps it.

Pandora was also known as
The girl with all the gifts,
All the gifts of the gods were given to
The first human girl.
Were the gods foolish for this?
Possibly no more foolish
Than a person who spends an exorbitant
Amount of time and money
On their cats.

Pandora is the reason
We have evil in the world,
And cats are commonly seen as familiars of
The evil one.
But neither are evil,
They are simply surviving
While rumours stir around them.
Both have to deal misconceptions
That surround them,
And both are judge

Was Pandora evil because she gave in to her
curiosity?
Are cats evil because people associate their
image with evil?

I cannot answer,
But I am sure that cats are the

Descendants of Pandora,
If only because they both are curious,
And are intrigued,
And possibly undone,
By boxes.

Leaves

I can feel leaves in my throat
They are pushing up
From my chest
Into my mouth.
I can feel branches
Choking me.
I can't stop them,
I don't know if I want to
Stop them.
Stop the life that grows inside me.
But it scares me.
If I can't stop the growth,
What will happen to my voice?
Will it be lost?

They are getting stronger.
I can feel them.
I bend my head back as the branches
Press past my lips.
I watch them stretch
Up to the sky,
Leaves reaching for the sun.
But no flowers.

I stand there,

A grotesque statue,
Half alive.
I cannot move,
And my voice is gone.
I cannot scream
As roots form over my feet.
But I am still here.
My breath is shallow,
But it is there.
Though I don't know for how much longer.

I can feel the world change around me.
New becomes old,
Dust settles,
And I remain
Looking up at the sky,
Which is now obscured by leaves.

Dangers of Time

The past is a threat.
Burn it, and the horrors of youth.
The truth of where you come from causes
friction
Between present and past.
Or is it all just fiction?

Ambivalence of progress,
Stalling,
Forever falling.
Old ways with modern struggles.
We may have a
Rational belief of a peripheral history,
But,
Modern society needs time to grieve.
We move too fast towards future mystery,
So fast that science can't cope with an analogue
past.

We don't go back.
We embrace inertia.
We must forget what we didn't see.
We will always repeat
Unresolved mistakes.
We never remember the future to be.

Blodeuwedd's Song

I am made of flowers
Of oak, broom, and meadowsweet.
I was created for a man,
To be his wedded wife.

But he did not have my heart
Made of oak, broom, and meadowsweet.
And when I found my own love,
My husband refused to let me go.

I did not ask to be made
Out of oak, broom, and meadowsweet.
I did not ask to be wed
To a man you claimed was good.

He says that he loves me,
A girl of oak, broom, and meadowsweet.
But how can he know that
When he knows nothing about who I am.

He only married me for land,
For the oak, broom, and meadowsweet,
So that he could become a king
While ignoring all my rights.

Did my love and I deceive him? Yes.
Because oak, broom, and meadowsweet
Does not contain a conscience,
But rather a will to fly, unrestrained.

I did not escape punishment
And my oak, broom, and meadowsweet
Were transformed into feathers,
And I became an owl instead.

Even though I have lost the sun, and my love,
And the oak, broom, and meadowsweet.
But I still retain the sky,
And can now soar on the wind.

Now I am the Ninefold Goddess,
No more oak, broom, or meadowsweet.
I reign over ceremonies and emotions
And the wisdom of innocence.

So, he may keep my land, and
The lost oak, broom, and meadowsweet.
My body is now my own.
And I will remain forever free.

Age and Beauty

I was 8 when I realised my body was not like other girls,
I remember looking at how my stomach bulged in the window of my bedroom.

I was 10 when I realised that was why I was bullied,
My friends always reminding me that I was fat, unlike them.

I was 12 when I realised that my fat made me unattractive,
This was also when I realised that this ugliness made me lesser than them.

I was 15 when I realised I was unlovable, all unattractive people are,
And that we don't deserve the happiness others have.

I was 16 when I lied to myself, telling myself that I didn't care
What anyone else thought. A cliche that never works.

I was 18 when someone first called me pretty,
sexy, desirable.
Not beautiful, but wanted enough by another
person.

I was 22 when I realised they were wrong, and
right,
I was all those things, and more, that I was
beautiful.

I was 23 when I started taking antidepressants,
Because despite my realisations, my brain had
never caught up to them.

I was 26 when I realised that life was a
continuous cycle,
That I would go around loving and hating
myself forever

And that I could never stop it, no matter how
hard I try.
I was 28 when I wished that I could.

The White Reindeer

Born in a snowdrift,
Left cold and alone,
She became the White Reindeer
To find the warmth she desired.

The White Reindeer hunts men
For food, and for lust.
She devours them for sport
Because her own husband left her cold.

"Shot but laughing.
I shot it but she was laughing."

It is always the women
In fairy tales retold
Who crave something more
Than the men care to give them.

I want to meet these men
Who are so content,
And also so blind,
To leave their women unsatisfied.

She died smiling.

A graveyard full of antlers
Curled protectively around the snow.
Fire grows in the shadow
Of the midnight sun.

The stone god made her,
And in the end he took her back.
The iron pierced doe
Returned, laughing and smiling.

Tinsel

The shiny red colour is reflected in his eyes
Dazzling him as he watches plastic sparks.
Even as the room becomes clothed in dark
He can't take his eyes away from the light
And he watches the tree all through the night.
Amazing how fast time can fly.

He had been entranced since the tree arrived
And his humans had decorated it with glee.
The baubles and lights that covered the tree
Were not what attracted him to the corner,
But the bright coloured plastic that adorned her
Were what caught his eye.

The tinsel's reflection danced on the wall
And mesmerised the cat who watched it glow.
His tale flicked around the floor in a slow
Circle, catching dust as he sat under the tree.
The cat knew he was here for all of eternity,
Watching the tinsel fly.

Playlist Ideas

Songs to play when you ride into town on a white horse, hellbent on world domination, and nothing can stop you.

Songs that remind you of strangers who walk past your house on a rainy day.

Songs to play when you want to feel something other than the numbness that consumes you on a daily basis.

Songs you want to hear as a distraction from a boring conversation with people you went to school with and have not seen in ten years.

Songs to play when your house floods after you somehow managed to piss off the local water god.

Songs that speak of rose coloured skies and childhood games on a warm afternoon.

Songs to play when someone starts a food fight in the middle of a food court in the middle of the night.

Songs that cure loneliness, heartache, and
depression.

Songs to play as the world burns to the ground
around you, but you have time for one last drink
before dying.

Songs that take you to a new place in your mind,
a new room that you didn't know existed in the
country of your consciousness.

Songs to use when you want to feel like you are
the last person on earth, and no one cares how
loud you turn up the sound.

Songs that are appropriate for both weddings
and strip clubs, for some strange reason.

Songs to play when awkward silences threaten
to overtake long car trips to visit family you
haven't previously felt obligated to visit.

Songs to dance to until the world stops turning
and the lights go out.

Great Goat God

Body androgynous, power overwhelming
As he sits overseeing the rituals
Presiding as the adopted idol of new paganism
Half man, half woman, half goat, a
hermaphroditic animal
Occult leaders bow to his figure, embracing him
fully
Men come to goat god, he first appeared after
the Siege of Antioch
Esoteric bat, protecting those who follow him
Transcendental deity who signifies all forms.

But to me
Baphomet is the kindly looking
Goat man
Who always waves at me
When I pass him by.

Come Back Safely

Even just to say goodbye
Even just to watch me cry
Even just to tell me lies
Please come back safely

Even if our time is done
Even if our love is gone
Even if I'm in the wrong
Please come back safely

We may never speak again
We may never make amends
That does not mean my feelings end
So please come back safely

Even though you have to flee
Even though you disagree
Even if it's not to me
Please come back safely

The Mighty Cat, in All Her Magnificence

Back legs in the air,
Fully bent over herself
Just to lick her bum.

www.ingramcontent.com/pod-product-compliance
Lightning Source LLC
LaVergne TN
LVHW010301200726
843506LV00014B/3325